EVERYTHING SPORTS ALMANACS

Sports Illustrated KIDS

ALL-PRO BASKETBALL ALMANAC

BY ELLIOTT SMITH

CAPSTONE PRESS
a capstone imprint

Published by Capstone Press, an imprint of Capstone
1710 Roe Crest Drive, North Mankato, Minnesota 56003
capstonepub.com

Library of Congress Cataloging-in-Publication Data is available on the Library of Congress website.

ISBN: 9798875232664 (hardcover)
ISBN: 9798875232619 (paperback)
ISBN: 9798875232626 (ebook PDF)

Summary: Exciting pro basketball facts in a variety of formats keep excited sports fans turning the page.

Editorial Credits
Editor: Mandy Robbins; Designer: Sarah Bennett; Media Researcher: Rebekah Hubstenberger; Production Specialist: Tori Abraham

Image Credits
Associated Press: Paul Vathis, 44; Getty Images: Adam Glanzman, 35, Alex Goodlett, cover (bottom left), Alex Slitz, 37 (middle right), Alvin Chung/Allsport, 41, Christian Petersen, 46, Darren McNamara/Allsport, 23, David Berding, 37 (top left), Emilee Chinn, 36 (middle), Ezra Shaw, 6, 21, Harry How, 18, iStock/envastudio (dots), throughout, Mark Blinch/NBAE, 26, Nathaniel S. Butler/NBAE, 17, Ronald Cortes, 37 (bottom left), Steph Chambers, 10 (bottom middle), Steve Dykes, 14, Thearon W. Henderson, 8 (bottom), 19, 24, Tim DeFrisco, 40 (top right), Todd Warshaw, 10 (bottom right), Tom Pennington, 47 (top left), Vincent Laforet/Allsport, 40 (bottom right); Shutterstock: adam_wasikowski, 7, Andrey Burmakin, 27, Armagadon, 12-13 (background), Brocreative (basketball hoop background), 15, 47, Fallen Knight (holographic background), cover and throughout, ffolas, 15 (top left), ghenadie (gold background), 16-17, 30-31, 34, grey_and (basketball), back cover, 20, 21, 25, HutagalungArt, 42-43 (background), kapona, 22, 45, kulyk, 28-29 (green background), Leremy, 8 (top right), mentalmind (trophy and gold stars), 33, 36, Naypong Studio (orange and blue basketball texture background), throughout, New Africa, 40 (measuring tape), Nurin Nabila A, 10-11 (background), onot, 9, StarLine, back cover (background), Volonoff (stars and bottom border), 30-31, 34; Sports Illustrated: Erick W. Rasco, cover (bottom right), 11, Hy Peskin, 4, John W. McDonough, 42, Manny Millan, cover (top), 5, 15 (bottom right), 16, 32, 39, Richard Meek, 12, 29, Robert Beck, 10 (middle left), Walter Iooss Jr., 13

All stats are current through April 1, 2025.

Printed in the United States 6504

Table of Contents

About the League

History and Growth

»The Minneapolis Lakers face the New York Knicks in 1954.

The National Basketball Association (NBA) was founded in 1949. It started with 17 teams. But in the 1950s, the league struggled to find fans. In 1954–55, the league was down to eight teams. But that season, the NBA introduced the 24-second shot clock. The game became much faster. Fans liked the quick action.

Still, the NBA trailed college basketball. That began to change in the 1980s. Superstars like Larry Bird, Michael Jordan, and Magic Johnson made the NBA explode in popularity. The league now has 30 teams. Top players from around the world test their skill in the NBA. More than 22 million fans watched NBA games in person during the 2023–2024 season.

»Clint Capela (#15) of the Atlanta Hawks drives to the basket in a 2024 game against the Sacramento Kings.

THE LONG, WINDING JOURNEY

Many NBA teams have moved. The reasons vary. Some are sold to new owners who want to relocate the team. Other teams moved because of poor attendance. The **Atlanta Hawks** and **Sacramento Kings** have had many stops en route to their current homes. Follow their journeys . . .

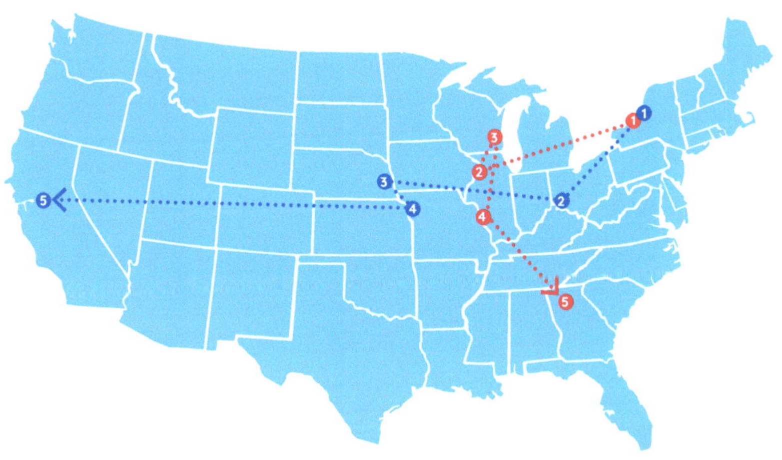

1. Buffalo Bisons (1946)
2. Tri-Cities Blackhawks (1946–1951)
3. Milwaukee Hawks (1951–55)
4. St. Louis Hawks (1955–1968)
5. **Atlanta Hawks** (1968–present)

1. Rochester Royals (1945–1957)
2. Cincinnati Royals (1957–1972)
3. Kansas City-Omaha Kings (1972–75)
4. Kansas City Kings (1975–1985)
5. **Sacramento Kings** (1985–present)

THE AMERICAN BASKETBALL ASSOCIATION

The American Basketball Association (ABA) formed in 1967. It was a direct challenge to the NBA. In 1976, the two leagues merged. Four ABA teams were accepted into the NBA—the New York Nets, Denver Nuggets, San Antonio Spurs, and Indiana Pacers.

Three-Pointer

The three-point line was adopted by the NBA in 1979. It was only supposed to be for one year as a test run. But the shot proved popular, and the league kept it. Boston Celtics' Chris Ford was the first player in league history to make a three-pointer.

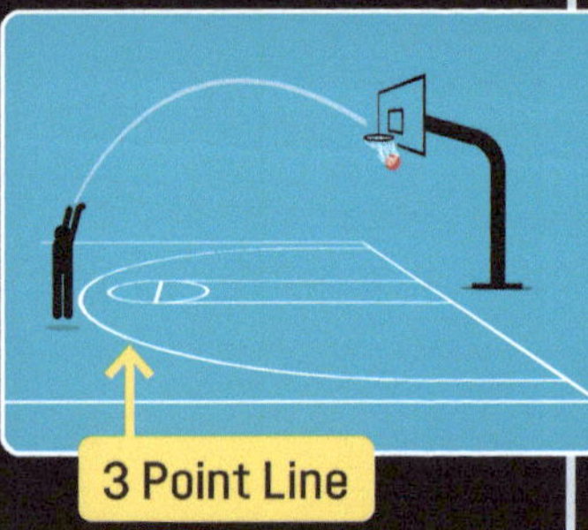

»Joel Embiid of the Philadelphia 76ers shoots from the three-point line against the Golden State Warriors in 2024.

ALL-TIME WINNING PERCENTAGES

These are the most successful teams in NBA history near the end of the 2024–25 season:

WINNING PERCENTAGE	TEAM
.596	Boston Celtics
.593	San Antonio Spurs
.592	Los Angeles Lakers
.541	Oklahoma City Thunder
.536	Phoenix Suns

RISE OF THE WNBA

As the NBA grew in popularity, so did women's basketball. The Women's National Basketball Association began in 1997 with eight teams.

The Houston Comets were the first WNBA dynasty, winning four straight championships. The league added more teams as the women's game found a larger fan base.

Players like Lisa Leslie (left), Sue Bird (center), and Cynthia Cooper (right) helped increase the WNBA's success.

In 2024, nearly 2.4 million people went to WNBA games. That was the league's highest attendance in 22 years!

»Indiana Fever Kelsey Mitchell takes a shot against the Los Angeles Sparks during a 2024 game.

The WNBA continues to add new teams. By 2026, the league will have 15 franchises.

The NBA's Earliest Stars

Bill Russell won 11 NBA championships with the Boston Celtics.

Jerry West

scored 27 points per game in his 14-year career.

George Mikan

won five NBA championships with the Minneapolis Lakers.

Oscar Robertson

was the first player in NBA history to average a triple-double for a season.

TRIPLE-DOUBLE

In basketball, a triple-double happens when a player reaches double digits in three of these five areas: points, rebounds, assists, blocks, and steals.

Greatest Games

DAME TIME

Damian Lillard is known for his clutch shooting. In the 2019 playoffs, Lillard's Portland Trail Blazers, held a 3–1 series lead against the Oklahoma City Thunder. One more win and the Blazers would advance to the next round.

With the game tied and less than five seconds left, overtime seemed likely. That's when Lillard launched a three-pointer from 37 feet (11.3 meters) away as the buzzer sounded. The ball swished through the net to give Portland a 118–115 victory. He finished the game with 50 points, and the phenomenon known as Dame Time was born.

0:00:00

Buzzer-Beaters

As of March 2025, there had been 840 buzzer-beaters in NBA history. That number is always growing!

» Phoenix Suns' Richard Dumas (21) in action against the Chicago Bulls during triple overtime in 1993

Triple Overtime

There have been only two triple-overtime NBA Finals games. Both involved the Phoenix Suns.

- The Boston Celtics beat the Suns 128–126 in 1976.
- The Suns defeated the Bulls 129–121 in 1993.

MJ'S GREATEST GAMES

Michael Jordan is the best NBA player of all time. His list of accomplishments is legendary. So were his big-game performances.

THE SHOT

Jordan nailed a fading buzzer-beater to give the Bulls a series win over the Cleveland Cavaliers in the 1989 playoffs.

THE SHRUG

Jordan hit six three-pointers in the first half of Game 1 of the 1992 NBA Finals. Even he was surprised! The camera caught Jordan shrugging in disbelief after he made the shot.

THE FLU GAME

Dealing with a stomach virus, Jordan scored 38 points, including the game-winning shot, to beat the Utah Jazz in the 1997 NBA Finals.

40 FOR 40

Four days after turning 40 years old, in February 2003, Jordan scored 43 points to lift the Washington Wizards to a victory over the New Jersey Nets. He became the first player over 40 to score more than 40 points in a game.

SCOREBOARD WORKOUT

Sometimes, an NBA game is so intense that it even gives the scoreboard a workout. Such was the case between the Sacramento Kings and Los Angeles Clippers on February 24, 2023.

The teams played a game that finished 176–175 in double overtime. The Kings won. It was the second-highest scoring game in NBA history.

» Malik Monk of the Sacramento Kings scores on a running jumper against the Los Angeles Clippers.

The Kings and Clippers combined for an NBA record 44 three-pointers. Three players—Malik Monk, De'Aaron Fox, and Kawhi Leonard—scored at least 40 points.

PLAYER	2-POINT SHOTS	3-POINT SHOTS	FREE THROWS	TOTAL POINTS
Malik Monk	9	6	9	45
De'Aaron Fox	15	2	6	42
Kawhi Leonard	10	6	6	44

THREE-POINT RECORD

Klay Thompson holds the NBA record of 14 three-pointers in one game. He scored 52 points to give the Golden State Warriors the win over the Chicago Bulls in October 2018.

DUNK HISTORY

The dunk is one of basketball's most exciting plays. It exploded in popularity during the 1980s, but it's been around as long as the game itself.

- The **first agreed-upon dunk** in organized basketball happened in 1936. Joe Fortenberry dunked in the Berlin Olympics, and the U.S. team won gold.
- The **first dunk in college** basketball occurred in 1944 by Oklahoma A&M's Bob Kurland.
- The NBA started the annual **Slam Dunk Contest** for All-Star Weekend in 1984. Slam stars such as Dominique Wilkins, Darryl Dawkins, and Vince Carter drew fan attention.
- Lisa Leslie registered the **first WNBA dunk** in 2002, and Brittney Griner has followed in her footsteps to be the **top female dunker**.

Mac McClung scored four perfect 50s in the 2025 AT&T Slam Dunk Contest. He became the first ever **three-peat dunk champion**.

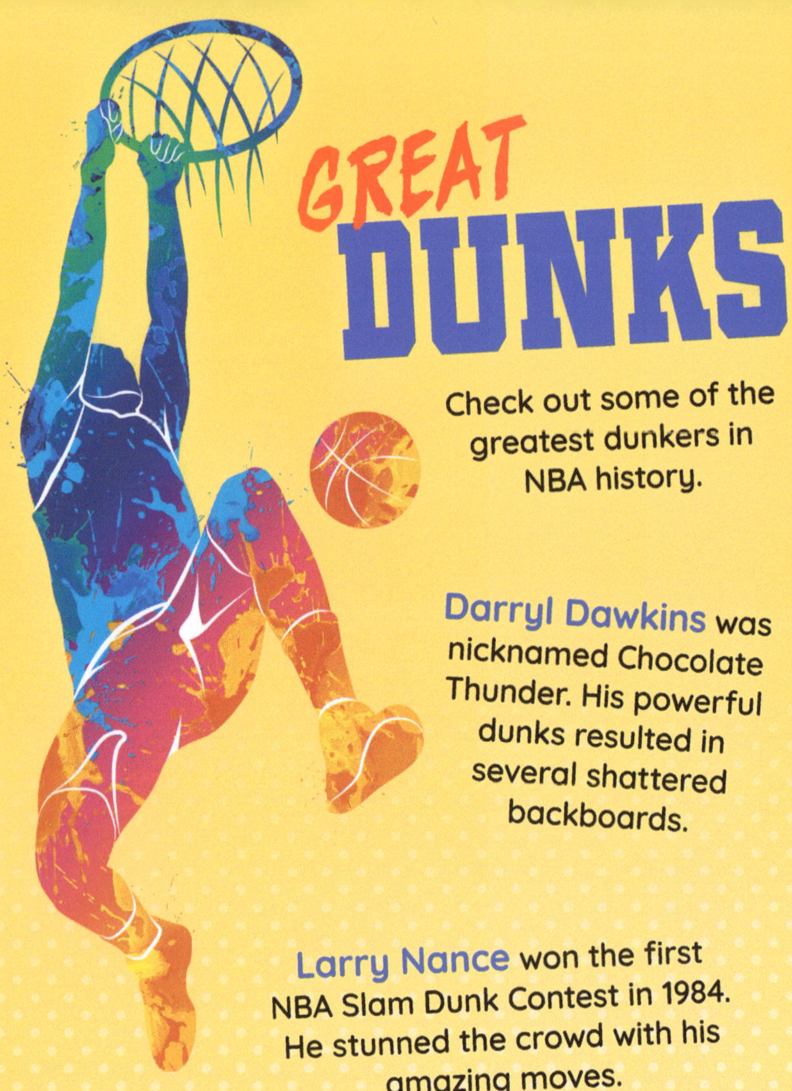

GREAT DUNKS

Check out some of the greatest dunkers in NBA history.

Darryl Dawkins was nicknamed Chocolate Thunder. His powerful dunks resulted in several shattered backboards.

Larry Nance won the first NBA Slam Dunk Contest in 1984. He stunned the crowd with his amazing moves.

Michael Jordan stunned fans at the 1988 Slam Dunk Contest. His performance made him a superstar and the dunk into the coolest move possible.

In the 2000 Olympics against France, **Vince Carter** shocked the world when he jumped over 7-foot, 2-inch (218.4-cm) Frederic Weis and threw down a powerful slam dunk.

BLOCK PARTY

LeBron James is one of the NBA's greatest players. In **Game 7 of the 2016 NBA Finals**, he proved why it always pays to hustle.

James's Cleveland Cavaliers were battling the Golden State Warriors. With just under two minutes left in a tie game, the Warriors had a 2-on-1 fast break. Warriors forward Andre Iguodala went up for a layup. It looked like a sure thing.

But James came sprinting down the court. **He leapt up and pinned Iguodala's shot against the backboard to keep the game tied.**

Golden State did not score another basket the rest of the game. Cleveland went on to win the NBA championship.

LOOOOOOOOONG SHOT!

Baron Davis holds the NBA record for the longest shot. In February 2001, Davis took the inbounds pass. With less than a second left, he flung the ball down the court. It swished in from 89 feet (27.1 m) away!

The Bounce

The 2019 Eastern Conference semifinals were a tough battle between the Philadelphia 76ers and Toronto Raptors. The series was tied at three going into Game 7. By the end of the second half, it was tied at 90–90. Raptors forward Kawhi Leonard launched a shot from the corner. Unbelievably, it bounced four times on the rim before falling through to give Toronto the buzzer-beating win.

»Fans and players watch keenly, waiting to see if Kawhi Leonard's shot will bounce in or out.

SHAQ'S SUPER SLAM

NBA legend Shaquille O'Neal was one of the game's biggest and strongest players. He showed his might in a game against the New Jersey Nets in April 1993. The Orlando Magic center received a pass. Shaq turned and slammed the ball so hard through the rim that the entire backboard collapsed.

O'Neal's brute force changed how NBA baskets were built. They were "Shaq-proofed" with reinforced steel braces. Additionally, any player who breaks the backboard is charged with a technical foul.

SEEING GREEN

The Boston Celtics were one of the NBA's original teams. In 1950, they hired coach Red Auerbach. He took over nearly every aspect of the organization. Auerbach slowly built one of the greatest dynasties in sports history.

Auerbach signed guard Bob Cousy and then drafted Bill Russell in 1956. The next season, the Celtics won their first title.

Two years later, the Celtics returned to the finals and won again. It was the first of eight straight NBA championships.

Auerbach named Russell to replace him in 1967. Russell became the first Black coach in any professional sport in 1967. He led Boston to two more championships in 1968 and 1969. When it was all over, the Celtics had won 11 championships in 13 seasons!

NOT ENOUGH FINGERS

Boston Celtics legend Bill Russell (number 6, left) had more NBA championship rings than fingers! The center won a record 11 championships during his career.

Great DYNASTIES

Minneapolis Lakers
1949–1954
5 championships

Boston Celtics
1957–1969
11 championships

Los Angeles Lakers
1980–88
5 championships

Chicago Bulls
1991–98
6 championships

Los Angeles Lakers
2000–02
3 championships

Golden State Warriors
2015–2022
4 championships

RUNNING of the BULLS

Michael Jordan was drafted by the Chicago Bulls in 1984. He took one of the worst teams in the league to the playoffs in his first year. Jordan was a global superstar, but it took help from players like Scottie Pippen and Steve Kerr to reach championship glory.

The Bulls won three straight titles from 1991–93. Jordan shocked the world by retiring in an attempt to play pro baseball. But when he returned to the game, the Bulls won three straight championships from 1996–98.

Thrill of Victory

Only four players have won a championship with three different teams.

PLAYER	TEAMS
Robert Horry	Houston Rockets, Los Angeles Lakers, San Antonio Spurs
LeBron James	Miami Heat, Cleveland Cavaliers, Los Angeles Lakers
John Salley	Detroit Pistons, Chicago Bulls, Los Angeles Lakers
Danny Green	San Antonio Spurs, Toronto Raptors, Los Angeles Lakers

WNBA Dynasties

Seattle Storm
4 championships
2004–2020

Houston Comets
4 championships
1997–2000
(Team no longer active)

Minnesota Lynx
4 championships
2011–2017

GOLDEN TOUCH

Most basketball experts thought Stephen Curry was too small to play in the NBA. He proved his doubters wrong. Thanks to the ability to shoot from anywhere on the court, Curry made the Golden State Warriors a modern NBA dynasty.

Coach Steve Kerr helped create an offense that played to Curry's strengths. Curry won two league Most Valuable Player (MVP) awards in 2015 and 2016.

With Curry's guard play, Klay Thompson's shooting, and Draymond Green's toughness, the Warriors found a key trio. They won four NBA titles in eight seasons from 2015–2022. Along the way, Golden State won 73 games in 2016, the NBA's best regular-season record.

»From left to right: Draymond Green, Klay Thompson, and Steph Curry

YOUNG STARS OF THE NBA/WNBA

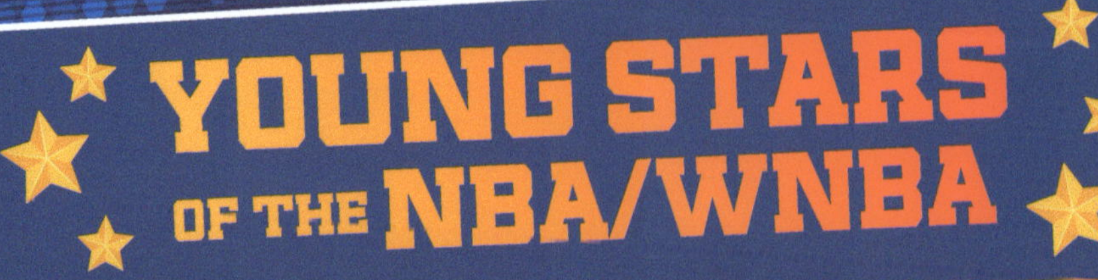

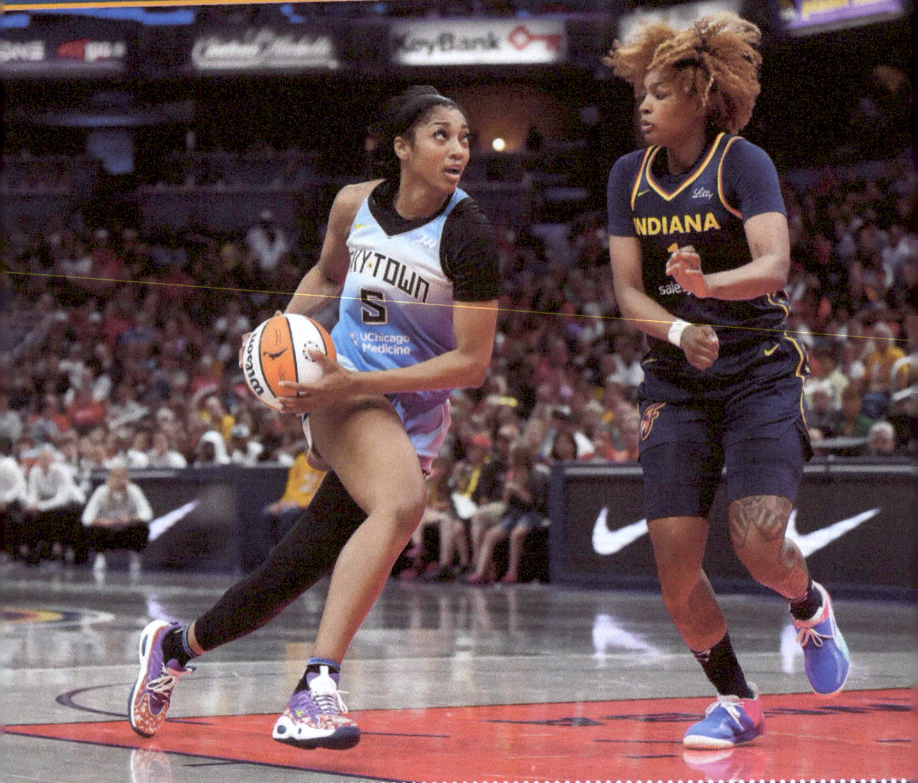

Angel Reese (above left) set the WNBA's double-double record (10 points, 10 rebounds) in her rookie season for the Chicago Sky in 2024.

The Minnesota Timberwolves' **Anthony Edwards** (above) is one of the league's most confident players and one of its best shooters.

Caitlin Clark (below) broke records in college and is now packing arenas in the WNBA for the Indiana Fever because of her amazing shooting skills.

Victor Wembanyama (left) of the San Antonio Spurs is a 7-foot, 3-inch (221-cm) center who is just as comfortable shooting three-pointers as he is blocking shots.

MAGIC AND BIRD

In the early 1980s, TV networks taped the NBA Finals and aired them at 11:30 pm Eastern Time. Back then, networks didn't think airing the games live would draw enough viewers. But Magic Johnson and Larry Bird helped change that.

The two players were college rivals. By 1979, they were both in the NBA. Johnson was on the Los Angeles Lakers, and Bird was on the Boston Celtics. Before long, both were fighting for NBA championships. Their popularity boosted the NBA's appeal as a whole. They became two of the most famous players in sports. Now, people wanted to see the big games live. The NBA Finals became a major event.

RIVAL STATS

Both players are in the NBA Hall of Fame.

Bird won three NBA titles and three league MVPs.

Magic captured five NBA titles and three MVPs.

THE LONG AND SHORT OF IT

It takes all sizes to play in the NBA. Here are some of the league's extremes:

Tallest Players in History:
7 foot, 7 inches
(234 centimeters)

Manute Bol
Washington Bullets, Philadelphia 76ers, Golden State Warriors, Miami Heat (1985–94)

Gheorge Muresan
Washington Bullets, New Jersey Nets (1993–2000)

Manute Bol

Average NBA Height:
6 foot 6.5 inches
(201 cm)

Shortest player in history:
5 foot 3 inches
(161 cm)

Tyrone "Muggsy" Bogues
Washington Bullets, Charlotte Hornets, Golden State Warriors, Toronto Raptors (1987–2001)

Muggsy Bogues

SKY HOOK

At 7 foot, 2 inches (218.4 cm), Kareem Abdul-Jabbar was so tall that college basketball outlawed dunks during his time at UCLA in the 1960s. So he developed the sky hook—a nearly unblockable shot. Abdul-Jabbar cradled the ball with one hand, jumped up, and flicked the ball over his head toward the hoop. Thanks to the sky hook, Abdul-Jabbar held the NBA's all-time scoring record for many years.

DYNAMIC DUO

»Shaq (left) and Kobe (right) in action against the Portland Trail Blazers during the 2001 playoffs

Shaquille O'Neal and Kobe Bryant were two of the NBA's greatest players. They began playing together for the Los Angeles Lakers in 1996. Both players wanted to be the number one option on the team. Neither wanted to give up the star role to the other player.

Legendary coach Phil Jackson convinced Bryant and O'Neal to work together when he took over the team in the 1999–2000 season. For three fantastic seasons, the pair were unstoppable. O'Neal's size and strength combined with Bryant's competitiveness and defense turned the Lakers into three-time champions.

But Shaq and Kobe's relationship fell apart over who was more important to the team. O'Neal was traded, while Bryant stayed with the Lakers.

KEEP IT 100

In 1962, one of the greatest NBA records was achieved. Philadelphia Warriors center Wilt Chamberlain scored 100 points. Chamberlain made 36 of 63 shots and 28 free throws. No footage exists of this landmark game. Its only evidence is an iconic photo taken of Chamberlain in a locker room holding a sign with "100" written on it. Kobe Bryant has the second highest point total. He scored 81 points in a 2006 game.

HIGHEST SCORING PLAYERS OF ALL TIME

PLAYER	TEAMS	YEARS PLAYED	POINTS SCORED
LeBron James	Cavaliers Heat Lakers	2003–present	James is the first NBA player to score 50,000 points and counting.
Kareem Abdul-Jabbar	Bucks Lakers	1969–1989	38,387
Karl Malone	Jazz Lakers	1985–2004	36,928
Kobe Bryant	Lakers	1996–2016	33,643

Queen of the WNBA

Diana Taurasi of the Phoenix Mercury was one of basketball's best scorers. The WNBA legend was the **number one pick** in the 2004 draft.

Taurasi was the league's **all-time** leading **scorer** with 10,646 points.

She's the only WNBA player to have scored more than **10,000 points**.

She holds **league records** for field goals, three pointers, and free throws.

Taurasi was **WNBA MVP** in 2009 and has won six Olympic gold medals.

In 2024, her **20th and final season**, Taurasi played in a career-high 36 games.

She averaged **18.8 points per game** throughout her entire career.

Most Seasons Played

Forward **Dirk Nowitzki** holds the NBA record for the most seasons played with one team. He started for the Dallas Mavericks for 21 seasons from 1998–2019.

Most Games in a Row

A.C. Green holds the NBA record for most consecutive games played. From November 1986 until he retired in April 2001, Green never missed a contest. He played in 1,192 straight games!

About the Author

Elliott Smith is a freelance writer, editor and author. He has covered a wide variety of subjects, including sports, entertainment, and travel, for newspapers, magazines and web sites. He lives in the Washington, D.C., area with his wife and two children.

More in This Series

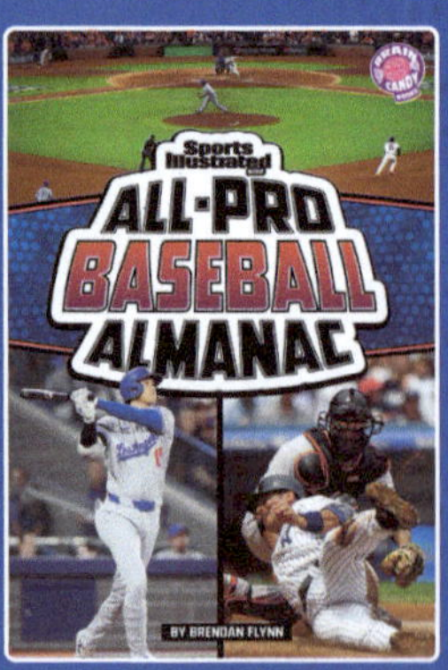

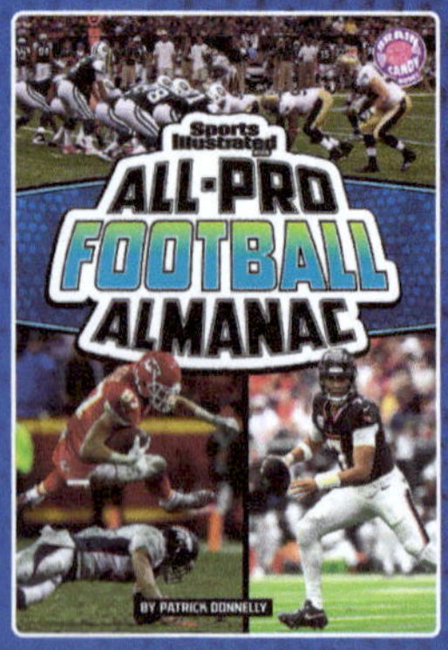

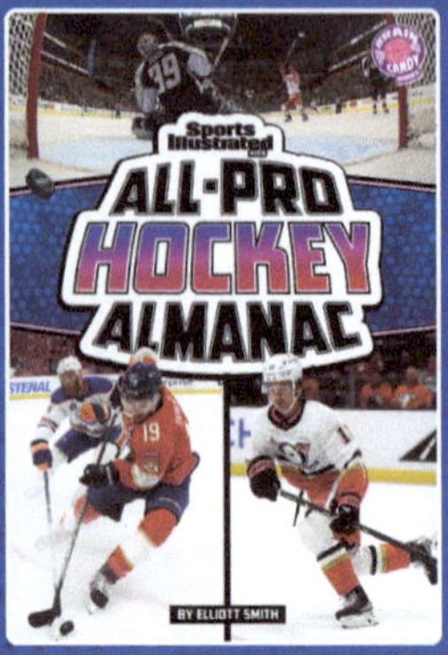

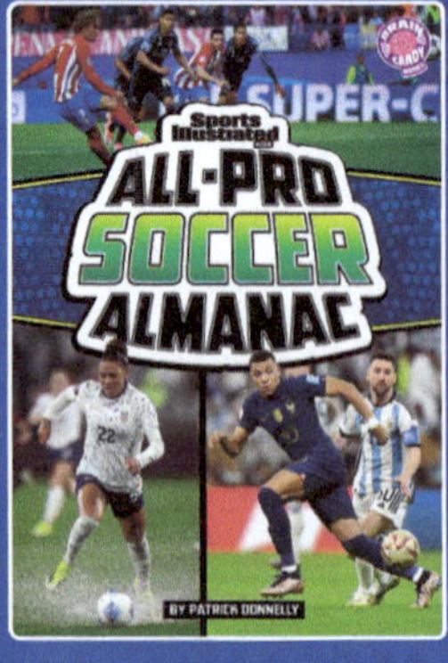

Decodable Words

am, at, mat, Sam, sat

High-Frequency Words

New: had, I, that, the, was

Review: [none]

Vocabulary Words

cat

dog

I sat.

I am the ________.

I had that.

I am the ________.

I am the **cat**.

cat

I had that.

I am the ________.

I am the cat mat.

I am the ________.

dog

I am the **dog**.

I was at the mat.

I am ______.

I had that.

I am ______.

I am Sam.

Build Background Knowledge

All animals need things to survive. They need water, food, shelter, and companionship. They find what they need in the environments where they live. As they live in a place, they change it. This book is about three living things: a cat, a dog, and Sam. What evidence can you find about what each one needs? What evidence can you find about how each one changes the environment?

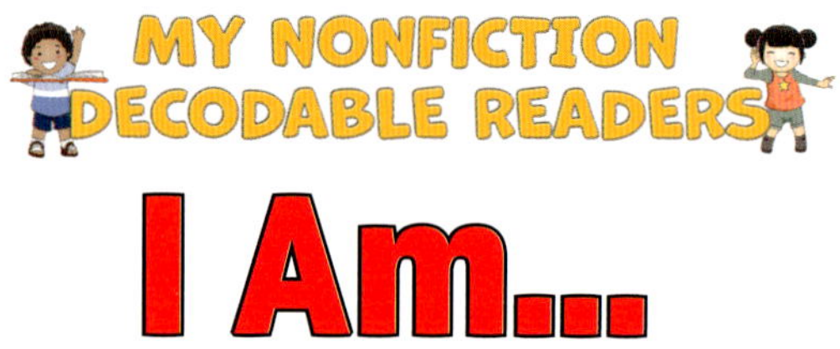

I Am...

Written by: Kim Thompson
Designed by: Rhea Magaro
Series Development: James Earley
Educational Consultant: Marie Lemke, M.Ed.

Photographs: All images from Shutterstock

Crabtree Publishing

crabtreebooks.com 800-387-7650

Printed in China/012024/FE20231222

Published in Canada
Crabtree Publishing
616 Welland Ave.
St. Catharines, Ontario
L2M 5V6

Published in the United States
Crabtree Publishing
347 Fifth Ave
Suite 1402-145
New York, NY 10016

Library and Archives Canada Cataloguing in Publication
Available at Library and Archives Canada

Library of Congress Cataloging-in-Publication Data
Available at the Library of Congress

Hardcover: 978-1-0398-4425-4
Paperback: 978-1-0398-4507-7
Ebook (pdf): 978-1-0398-4584-8
Epub: 978-1-0398-4654-8
Read-Along: 978-1-0398-4724-8
Audio: 978-1-0398-4794-1